the BAD GUYS

EPISODE

3

THE FURBALL STRIKES BACK

SCHOLASTIC

PUBLISHED IN THE UK BY SCHOLASTIC, 2023
1 LONDON BRIDGE, LONDON, SE1 9BG
SCHOLASTIC IRELAND, 89E LAGAN ROAD, DUBLIN INDUSTRIAL ESTATE,
GLASNEVIN, DUBLIN, D11 HP5F

TEXT AND ILLUSTRATIONS © AARON BLABEY, 2016
FIRST PUBLISHED BY SCHOLASTIC PRESS, A DIVISION OF SCHOLASTIC AUSTRALIA IN 2016
THIS COLOUR EDITION FIRST PUBLISHED IN 2023

ISBN 978 0702 32598 4

A CIP CATALOGUE RECORD FOR THIS BOOK IS AVAILABLE FROM THE BRITISH LIBRARY.

PRINTED BY BELL AND BAIN LIMITED, GLASGOW
PAPER MADE FROM WOOD GROWN IN SUSTAINABLE FORESTS AND OTHER CONTROLLED
SOURCES.

1 3 5 7 9 10 8 6 4 2

DESIGN BY NICOLE STOFBERG. COLOUR BY SARAH MITCHELL

WWW.SCHOLASTIC.CO.UK

AARON BLABEY

WITH COLOUR BY SARAH MITCHELL

the BAD GUYS

EPISODE 3

THE FURBALL
STRIKES BACK

HEROES OR VILLAINS?

A SPECIAL REPORT BY

TIFFANY FLUFFIT

They are the **MONSTERS** that haunt our darkest nightmares . . .

RE-ENACTMENT

Or ARE they?

Well, not according to THIS chicken . . .

SUNNYSIDE CHICKEN FARM was a terrible place. We spent our whole lives locked in tiny cages. But then that wonderful wolf and his friends—they set us free!

BROOKE

But . . . didn't one of them try to EAT you?

Yes. But he spat me back out again.

IS THIS CHICKEN *CRAZY?*

And Brooke is not the only one to claim that these VILLAINS are actually . . .

HEROES IN DISGUISE!

Every one of the 10,000 chickens set free from Sunnyside has told the same story.

POLICE REPORT

Sunnyside

SHOULD MUTANT SARDINES BE ALLOWED TO WALK THE STREETS?

I thought they were lovely.
Especially the really big chicken.
Or maybe he was a shark.
It was hard to tell . . .

PAT. HOMEMAKER.

They inspired me to
follow my dreams.
I'll never forget them.

FIONA. CELEBRITY CHEF.

We must all be careful not to judge others
simply by the way they *look*. Sometimes
the scariest-looking creatures can be the
kindest and best of all.

DIANE. SUPREME COURT JUDGE.

So, can ALL these chooks be **CRAZY?**

Or are those

HORRIFYING CREATURES

actually . . . trying to do good?

Are they out there doing good deeds?

Or are they **LURKING OUTSIDE YOUR DOOR**, waiting for a chance to show us that they're nothing but a bunch of . . .

... BAD GUYS?!

• CHAPTER 1 •

IF YOU GO DOWN TO THE WOODS TODAY...

Hey, chico, can you slow down? I don't feel so good . . .

NO CAN DO, Mr Piranha. There's NO TIME TO LOSE!

Legs! Are we nearly there?

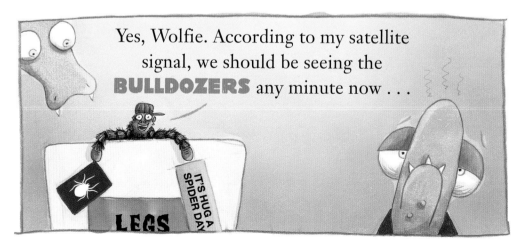

Yes, Wolfie. According to my satellite signal, we should be seeing the **BULLDOZERS** any minute now . . .

Great! So, let's go over the plan ONE MORE TIME.

If you tell us the plan one more time, I'm going to bite you on the butt.

WE KNOW THE PLAN!

Hey! Take it easy, Mr Snake. This is important.

So anyway . . . I got an **ANONYMOUS CALL** telling me that way out here in **THE WOODS**, there's a bunch of **BULLDOZERS** getting ready to smash up the homes of a lot of **CUTE, FURRY ANIMALS**.

And we're here to make sure

THAT DOESN'T HAPPEN.

WE KNOW ALREADY!

Oh man . . . I don't feel good AT ALL . . .

MR SHARK!

What?

Where's your disguise?

Oh yeah.
I forgot.

See?! **THIS** is why I
keep repeating the plan!

Yeah, yeah.
Whatevs.

Hey! Who's
THAT guy?!

 **WE KNOW THE PLAN!**

Uh-oh. Stop the car . . .

WE'VE BEEN OVER IT A **MILLION** TIMES AND WE **KNOW THE PLAN!**

 **STOP THE CAR!**

 **SCREEECH!**

 What's wrong?!

Where are YOU going?

I need to do 'number twos'.

You need to do *WHAT*?!

Car travel upsets my tummy.

Are you serious?!
The bulldozers are
RIGHT THERE!

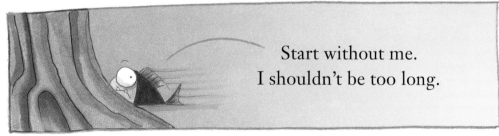

Start without me.
I shouldn't be too long.

Well . . . if you've gotta go . . .

You got it.
If anything moves within
1000 yards, I'll see it.

All right.
It's time to
be HEROES.

Do you have to say
that EVERY time?

LET'S ROCK!

Um . . . guys . . . ?

Um . . . my sensors are picking up something weird about those bulldozers, dudes . . .

Um . . .

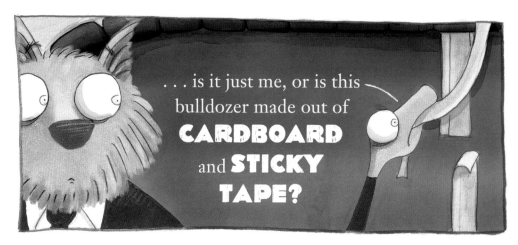

. . . is it just me, or is this bulldozer made out of **CARDBOARD** and **STICKY TAPE?**

Hey, that's weird . . .

Why would someone get us all the way out here if the bulldozers weren't real?

My car!

LEGS!

Hey, does anyone else think the ground feels weird?

Phew!
I wouldn't go behind **THAT**
tree anytime soon . . .

Hey . . .
What'd I miss?

the · CHAPTER 2 ·
LAIR OF DR MARMALADE

Wha . . . ?

Well, HELLO, genius.
Nice of you to join us . . .

We're tied up!

Oh, really? Thanks.
WE HADN'T NOTICED!

But who would do this?

Who *wouldn't* do this?
We're **BAD** guys, man.
Guys like us don't get a
happy ending.

NO!

There must have
been a mistake!
**WE'RE
HEROES!**

Wait a minute! I know you!

You're that cute little
guinea pig from the old
house next to Sunnyside . . .
You're MARMALADE!

That's **DOCTOR**
Marmalade to you!

Forgive me.

Allow me to
introduce myself . . .

Billionaire mad scientist?!
He's a **GUINEA PIG!**

So what?! Just because I'm a guinea pig, I CAN'T BE A **BILLIONAIRE MAD SCIENTIST?**

Oh. Well, no . . . I suppose you could be . . .

It's true!
I **AM** a billionaire!
And I **AM** a scientist!

But am I **MAD?!**
Hmmm,
I wonder . . .

AM I
MAD?!

You blew up Legs!
You're a monster!

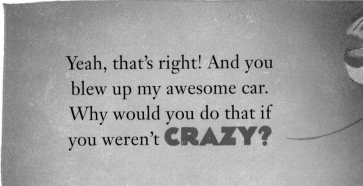

Yeah, that's right! And you blew up my awesome car. Why would you do that if you weren't **CRAZY?**

Well, let me think.

Hmmm, yes. Tell me . . . Did you think you could just **BREAK INTO** one of my **CHICKEN FARMS** and steal **10,000 CHICKENS** and I'd just be

COOL WITH THAT?!

YOUR chicken farm?
But you're just a guinea pig!

YOU'RE STILL NOT GETTING IT—

I'M A BILLIONAIRE MAD SCIENTIST WHO **OWNS A LOT OF CHICKEN FARMS** AND

I'M VERY ANGRY WITH YOU!

Hang on. Are you saying that you blew up our car and strung us up **JUST** because we rescued those chickens?

FINALLY!
Yes, that's right.

But you're *not* mad about all the **BAD** stuff we've done in our lives?

No.

So that means . . .

YOU BET I DO!

THIS RIDICULOUS HERO THING HAS CAUSED US NOTHING BUT TROUBLE AND

I'VE HAD ENOUGH!

Hey!

WHAT?!

I think you have failed to notice my beautiful new toy. Isn't it LOVELY?

Cool. A big red button. What's it do?

Oh, nothing much . . .

It's just going to **DESTROY YOU** and help me **TAKE OVER THE ENTIRE WORLD!**

HE HE HE HE HE!

You know what?
I don't think I like that guinea pig.

• CHAPTER 3 •
DO YOU SEE WHAT I SEE?

Hey! Chicos!
Where is everybody?
It's not my fault I
needed to poop!

VOOMP!

Shhh!

¡Ay, caramba! What happened to you?!

I jumped from the car one millisecond before it was **BLOWN TO PIECES BY A LASER CANNON** and then I watched the rest of the gang get **SUCKED INTO THE BOWELS OF THE EARTH.**

Oh. Cool.

WHAT?!

It was a **TRAP**, Mr Piranha.
The bulldozers weren't real. I think
someone got us out here deliberately
and I think Wolf and the guys have
been **CAPTURED!**

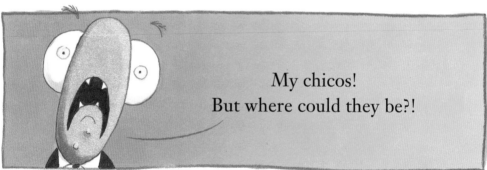

My chicos!
But where could they be?!

Look over there . . .

Sunnyside?!
But what's a chicken farm doing out
here in the middle of the woods?

Exactly!
Fishy, don't you think?

Hey! Who are you calling 'Fishy'?
And yes, I DO think.

Um . . . OK. Anyway . . .
We need to get inside that
building, and I have a plan . . .

Cock-a-doodle-doo!

Huh?

Hmmm.
Weird.

Give us a kiss.

FAINT!

Wow. He's out cold. You really do freak everyone out, don't you?

Yep. Always have . . .

. . . always . . . will . . .

Hey!

What?

I think . . . I just saw . . .

. . . a **NINJA!**

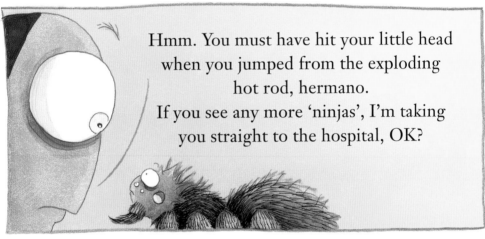

Hmm. You must have hit your little head
when you jumped from the exploding
hot rod, hermano.
If you see any more 'ninjas', I'm taking
you straight to the hospital, OK?

Because I don't know what
we'll find in here, chico. But I'll
promise you one thing . . .

There won't be
any ninjas . . .

the MIND OF A MONSTER

So! Now that I have your attention, I'm going to tell you a little story.

Once upon a time,
there was an itty, bitty guinea pig who got

SICK

of everyone saying how
CUTE and **CUDDLY** he was.

So he decided to do something about it . . .

First of all, he made billions of dollars putting chickens in cages, but somehow that just wasn't enough.

SO! He created a **SECRET WEAPON** that would make sure **NO-ONE EVER** called him **CUTE** and **CUDDLY** again. A weapon **SO POWERFUL** that it would change the world forever with the push of a button . . .

THIS BUTTON!

But what's wrong with being
cute and cuddly?
I wish *I* was cute and cuddly!
Everyone **LOVES** guinea pigs.

I don't want *love*,
you ridiculous fish.

And now that I have it, there's

NOTHING

any of you can do to take it away
from me!

HEHE
HEHEHE!

Ahhh . . . sorry. Can you
just give us a second?

What?
Erm . . . all right.
But don't take long, OK?

OK. So the guinea pig is out of his mind. What do we do?

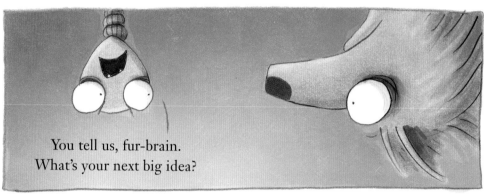

You tell us, fur-brain. What's your next big idea?

Listen, Snake, you'd better start helping out here or—

OR WHAT?

Guys, cut it out.

OR YOU'LL BE **SORRY**, YOU NASTY LITTLE **OVERGROWN SLUG!**

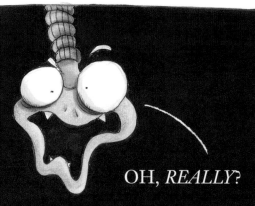

OH, *REALLY*?

AND WHAT ARE YOU GOING TO DO?

ARE YOU GOING TO

BORE ME TO DEATH

WITH YOUR NEXT IDIOTIC PLAN TO TURN US ALL INTO **GOODY-GOODY GUMDROPS?!**

THAT'S YOUR LAST WARNING, SNAKE.

You both need to stop arguing. It's starting to really UPSET me . . .

Warning, schmorning! Do your worst, you dimwitted **HERO WANNABE!**

THAT'S IT!

DON'T DO IT, WOLF.

TOO LATE!

MUNCH!

Let me out of here right now!

Hey! Did he just
eat the snake?!

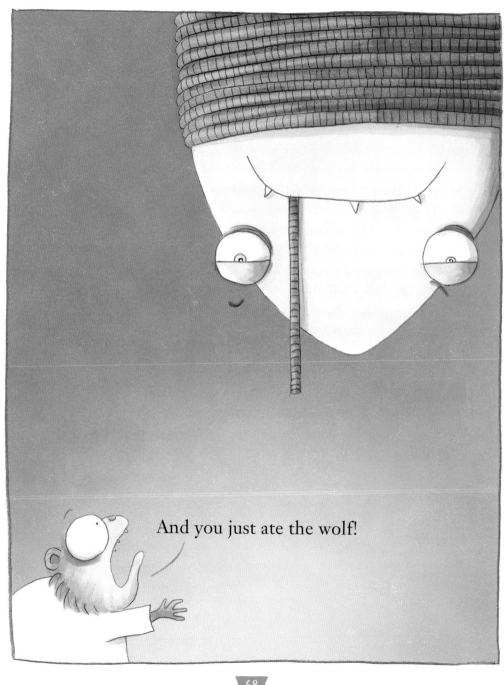

And you just ate the wolf!

I'm warning you, Wolf! Cough me up!

Not a chance, Slimy.
Shark! I'm NOT going to ask you again!

Wait a minute! Are you inside the shark?!

None of your business!

But that means I'm inside a wolf AND a shark!

Tell someone who cares!

This is like being trapped inside some kind of really
disgusting Russian doll and I DON'T LIKE IT!

Big whoop.
Shark, I'm going to count to ten . . .

You wouldn't
BELIEVE
what I have to put up with.

· CHAPTER 5 ·
SURPRISE, SURPRISE

Oh, man! There are guards everywhere!
How are we ever going to find them?

Hey, look!
Down there!

It's Shark!

NO-ONE TIES UP MY CHICOS AND GETS AWAY WITH IT! LET'S CUT THAT ROPE **RIGHT NOW!**

NIBBLE!

NIBBLE!
NIBBLE!

Mr Piranha?

Yeah, kid? What is it?

NIBBLE!
NIBBLE!

I know this sounds crazy
. . . but I really do think
I saw a ninja.

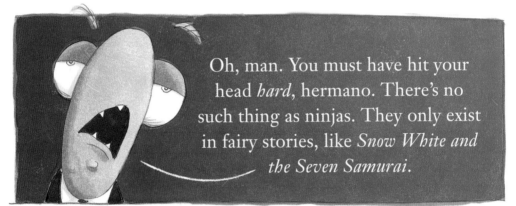

Oh, man. You must have hit your
head *hard*, hermano. There's no
such thing as ninjas. They only exist
in fairy stories, like *Snow White and
the Seven Samurai*.

Actually,
I'm pretty
sure that's
not true . . .

FREEZE!

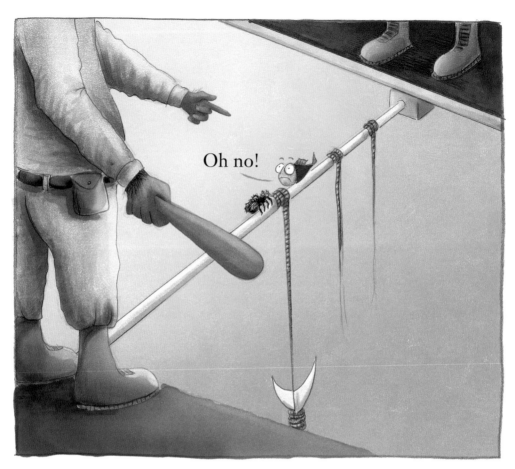

Oh no!

SHARK! I'm sorry!
They caught us!

Piranha?! Is that you?

Oh yes. I forgot to mention—your silly little friends thought they could sneak in here and rescue you! Isn't that *adorable*?

It seems that none of you fully understand how much danger you're in.

Oh well. I guess I'll just

UNLEASH THE END OF THE WORLD AS WE KNOW IT!

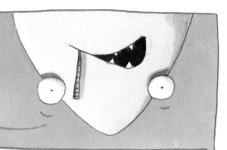

If you don't mind me saying, you seem like a very troubled guinea pig.

You have NO idea.

NOW LET'S GET THIS PARTY STARTED!

PIRANHA! RUN!

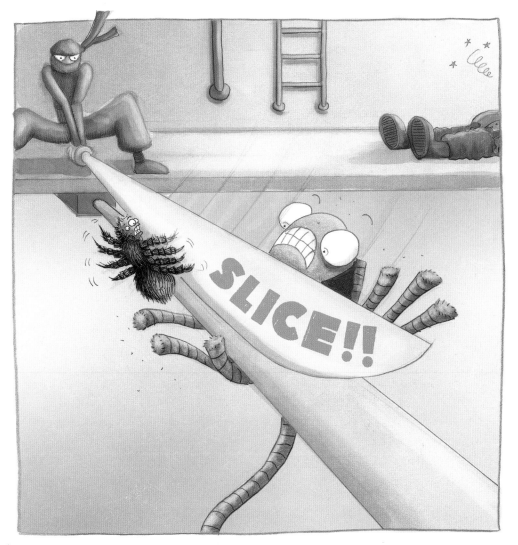

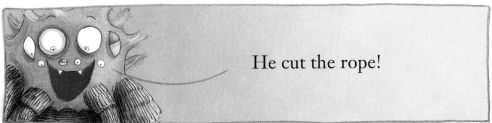

He cut the rope!

SPLAT!

DONK!

Hey, man.
Thanks.
You broke
my fall.

OK. Does someone want to tell me what's going on here?

Certainly, Mr Wolf . . .

LEGS!
YOU'RE
ALIVE!

FLING!

FLING!

So, tell me . . .

· CHAPTER 6 ·
the
SECRET AGENT

Who **ARE** you?

My name is

SPECIAL AGENT FOX,

Mr Shark.
And I'm very pleased
to meet you.

I'm afraid you boys have stumbled into a very dangerous situation.

Doctor Rupert Marmalade is one of the most **DESPICABLE VILLAINS** on the face of the earth. We've been on his tail for years, trying to catch him in the act.

It seems we've finally done it.

We? Who's *we?*

I'm an agent for the

INTERNATIONAL LEAGUE OF HEROES.

We're a secret global organisation sworn to protect the earth from evil.

And that is what we do.

Hey! That's kind of what *we* do, isn't it, Wolfie?

We are the . . .
Good Guys Club,
Agent Fox . . .
at your service . . .
hehehe . . . hehehe
. . . ah . . . yup . . .
gughhhh . . .

The 'Good
Guys Club'?
Is that what you
call yourselves?

Yep. We sat up ALL NIGHT
trying to think of the
STUPIDEST NAME in
the HISTORY OF **STUPID**
NAMES and—**BAM!**—
there it was.

Oh, I don't know.
I think it's rather cute.

But I'm afraid you're a little
out of your depth here, boys.

Your antics at the chicken farm made old Doctor Marmalade here

OBSESSED

with you. But don't worry. We'll soon have him safely locked up, won't we, Marma—

Oh dear.

Has anyone seen where the supervillain went?

Right here, Agent Fox.

Whoops. That's unfortunate.

And I DO hope you enjoy the **END OF THE WORLD!**

Hehe!

CLUNK!

MY **SECRET WEAPON** HAS BEEN RELEASED AND IT'S **ON ITS WAY!** CAN YOU GUESS WHAT IT IS?

HEHE HE!

Oh, and just to make things a little more interesting . . .

THIS BUILDING WILL SELF-DESTRUCT IN 90 SECONDS . . . 89! 88! 87! 86!

76! 75! 74! 73!

Hmm. The old disappearing-up-a-great-big-bendy-tube trick. That's disappointing.

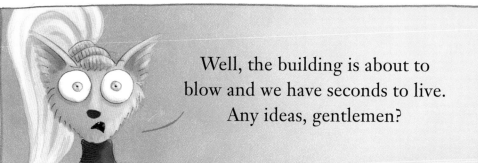

Well, the building is about to blow and we have seconds to live. Any ideas, gentlemen?

· CHAPTER 7 ·
LEARNING TO RIDE A BIKE

Climb aboard, everyone, and I'll get you out of here.

We won't all fit on one motorbike!

Hmm. You could be right. I don't suppose any of you can ride one of these . . . ?

Marvellous.
Well, you take Mr Snake and
I'll get the others to safety.

Good luck,
Mr Wolf.

PECK!

32! 31!

30! 29!

We'll see you outside, gentlemen!

REV! REV!

Byyyyeeee!

I didn't know you could ride a motorbike.

I just didn't want to disappoint her.

You know what?

What?

Let's just . . .

FANG IT!

Wow. You have a very
unusual style, Mr Wolf.
Very impressive.

But I'm afraid things are
going to be a little more
difficult than we thought.

Oh, really? Why's that?

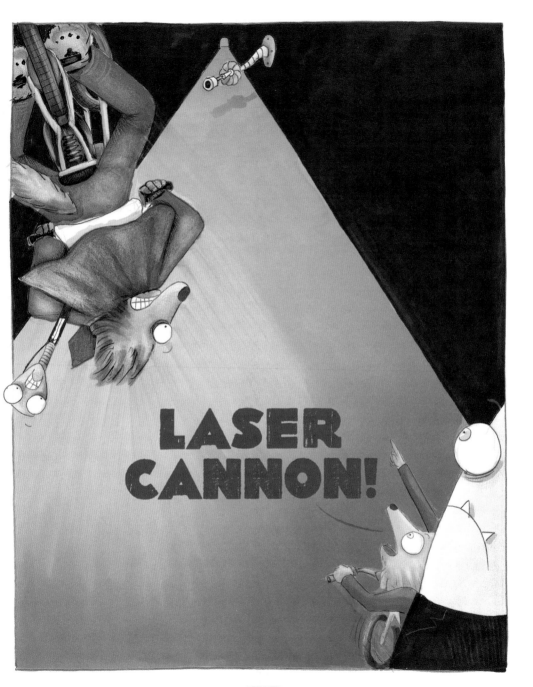

Wow. He really is awfully brave, isn't he?

Well, yes. In Bolivia, we have a name for people like that . . .

We call them 'idiots'.

I HATE YOU, WOLF!

WELL, I **DON'T** HATE YOU, SNAKE!

AND I **WON'T GIVE UP ON YOU**, NO MATTER WHAT HAPPENS.

I'M SORRY I **ATE** YOU EARLIER. BUT I'M **NOT** SORRY FOR GETTING YOU INTO ALL THIS TROUBLE.

THIS IS WHAT HEROES DO.

AND I TRULY BELIEVE **YOU HAVE A HERO INSIDE YOU**, MR SNAKE.

AND I'LL NEVER STOP BELIEVING THAT. **EVER**.

You're crazy. And you're going to get us all killed.

MAYBE!

BUT NOT TODAY!

THIS BUILDING WILL SELF-DESTRUCT IN 10 SECONDS . . . 9! 8! 7! 6! 5!

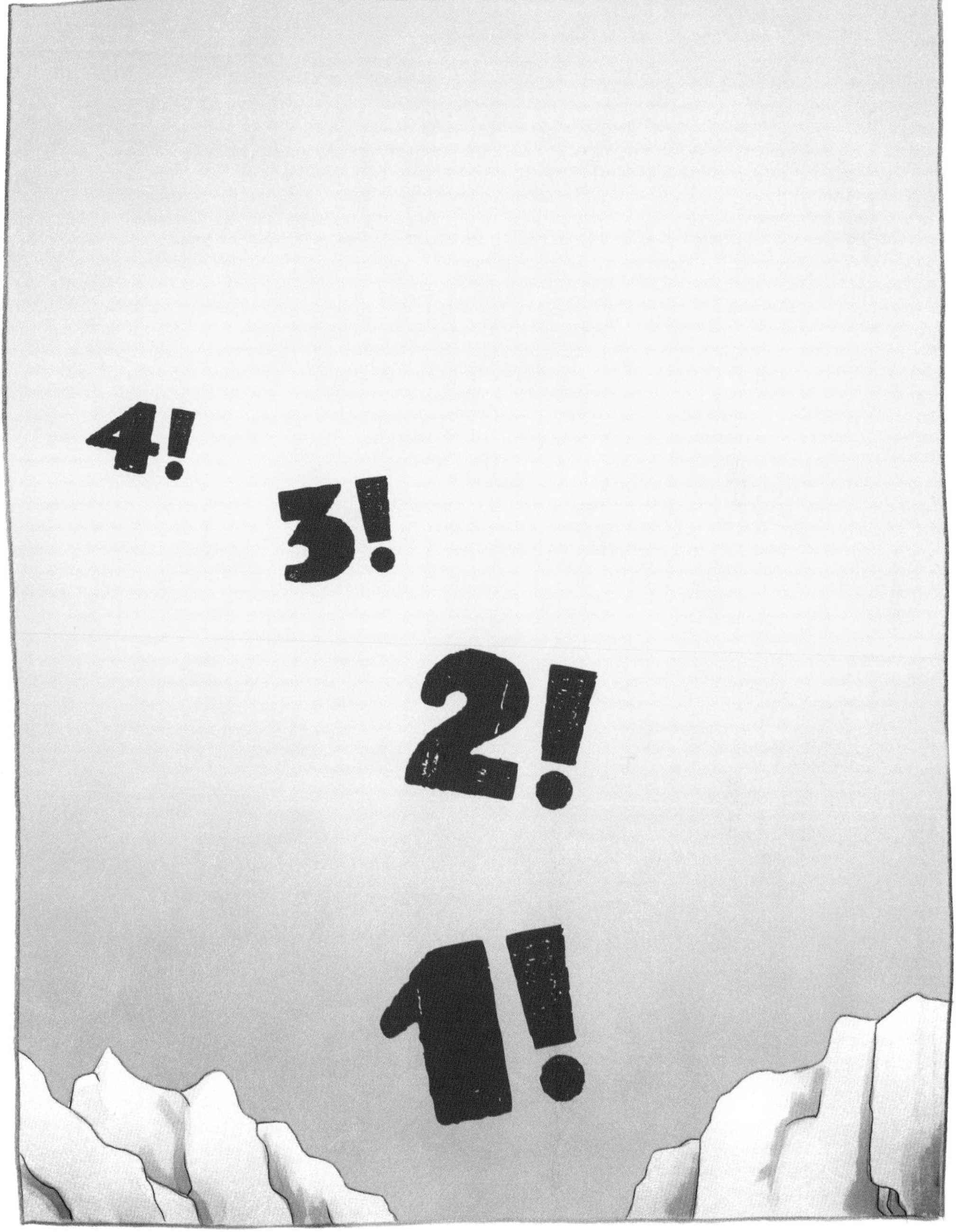
4!
3!
2!
1!

· CHAPTER 8 ·
A LITTLE FAVOUR

Tricked you!
The building wasn't
REALLY going to blow up!

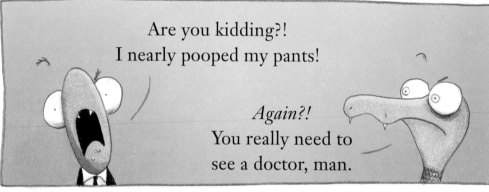

Are you kidding?!
I nearly pooped my pants!

Again?!
You really need to
see a doctor, man.

YOU DIDN'T
REALLY THINK
I'D BLOW UP MY
**SECRET
WEAPON,**
DID YOU?

I'm getting sick of this.
WHAT 'Secret Weapon'?
I'll bet it's just another trick!

Hmmm.
Well, you just wait a few minutes,
Mr Wolf, and see what comes out
of this tunnel!

TODAY IS
THE END OF
CUTE AND
CUDDLY . . .
FOREVER!

I really don't like
that guinea pig.

Nor do I, Mr Wolf.
And that's why I need
to ask you a favour.

Anything!

I need to follow
Marmalade
RIGHT NOW.
But someone
needs to stay here
and deal with his
**SECRET
WEAPON**.

Any minute now, something **TRULY TERRIFYING** will come out of that tunnel and I need some heroes to be standing guard when it does.

Will **YOU** be my heroes, gentlemen?

Will you help me
SAVE THE WORLD?

Um . . . I'm really not sure . . .

I actually have a hair
appointment to get to . . .

I'd love to help, señorita, but I'm afraid
I need to find a clean pair of pants . . .

Sister, you're out of your mind . . .

OF COURSE WE WILL!

Thank you, Mr Wolf.
I'm counting on you, boys.

We all are.

Oh great.
Now she's counting on us.

Well, I've got a villain to catch!

She's even got

ROCKET BOOTS!

Yes, there are quite a few perks to being a hero, Mr Wolf.

Oh, and Mr Snake?

Yeah?

I know what you did at the chicken farm. **YOU** are the reason those chickens are free. You're ALREADY a hero.

You just have to start *believing* it.

Good luck, boys!

ZOOOOM!

• CHAPTER 9 •
CUTE AND CUDDLY NO MORE

Did you hear that?

Yeah. There's something moving around in there . . .

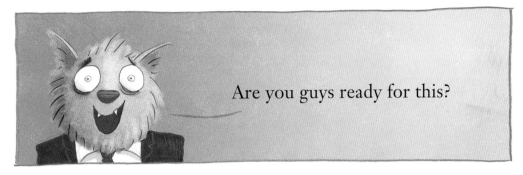

Are you guys ready for this?

NO.

Fair enough.
I'm not sure I am either.
But it doesn't matter,
does it? Because we have
a job to do. It's up to us
to protect the world.

It's up to us—

THE GOOD
GUYS CLUB.

Seriously, man, now that we've heard about the **INTERNATIONAL LEAGUE OF HEROES**, our name sounds so lame it makes me wish I had hands—so I could **SLAP YOU**.

Really?
You don't like our name?

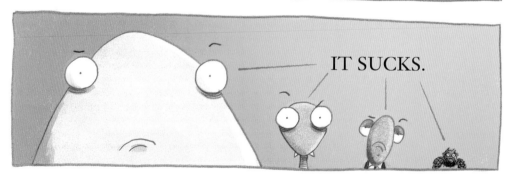

IT SUCKS.

OK . . .well . . .
We **ARE** helping the awesome League of Heroes, right now . . .

So that kind of makes us awesome too, doesn't it?

Kind of.

Well then, Kind-Of-Awesome-League-Of-Good-Guys-Guys, let's show this SECRET WEAPON what we're made of!

Hey! **HAHAHAHA!**
Everybody relax!
LOOK!
IT'S JUST ANOTHER **TRICK!**
IT'S JUST A BUNCH OF . . .

Phew!
Well, **THAT'S** a relief!

No, no, no . . . wait a minute . . .
There's something **WEIRD**
about those kittens.
Why are they **LIMPING?**
And **MOANING?**
And . . . **DROOLING?**

NO!
IT CAN'T BE!
IT IS!
IT'S . . .
**IT'S AN ARMY
OF . . .**

137

It's a **ZOMBIE KITTEN APOCALYPSE!**

Should you **panic**? Should you **cry**?

Should you **poop your pants**?

NO! You should sit back and watch the **FUR FLY** as the world's **BADDEST GOOD GUYS** take on **MAD MARMALADE'S MEOWING MONSTERS!**

You'll **laugh till you cry**. Or **laugh till you fart**. (It doesn't matter which, it's totally your choice.)

Just don't miss . . . *the BAD GUYS*

EPISODE **4** **IN FULL COLOUR**

COMING SOON!